ANIMALS
AND THEIR
BABIES

CATS
AND KITTENS

by Annabelle Lynch

Contents

Growing Inside	2
Being Born	4
Newborn Kittens	6
Meow!	8
Feeding First	10
On the Move	12
Grooming	14
Super Senses	16
New Homes	18
Grown-Up Cats	20
A Cat's Life Cycle	22
Word Bank	23
Index	24

A+

Smart Apple Media

GROWING INSIDE

Cats have babies called kittens.
Kittens grow inside their mothers.

A mother's tummy gets **bigger** and **bigger!**

BEING BORN

ZZZZ

After around nine or 10 weeks, the kittens are ready to be born.

The mother cat finds somewhere warm and safe to have its babies.

Cats usually
have between three
and five kittens at a time.
This is called a litter of kittens.

NEWBORN KITTENS

Newborn kittens can't see or hear. Their eyes are closed, and their ears stay folded down.

Snuggle up!

Newborn kittens get cold easily. They have to stay close to their mothers to keep **warm.**

6

After a few days, kittens start
to hear sounds. After about 10 days,
they open their eyes.

All kittens have
blue eyes at first.

MEOW!

Kittens can cry out almost as soon as they are born. These cries sound like little squeaks!

squeak! squeak!

The sounds let the mothers know that the kittens are **hungry** or **cold**.

As they grow up, kittens can meow for attention. When they are happy, they might purr. When they are scared, they might **hiss!**

9

FEEDING FIRST

Newborn kittens feed only on **milk** from their mothers' teats.

After a few weeks, kittens have grown their baby teeth. They are now ready to eat soft food.

Yum!

They can feed as often as once an hour!

ON THE MOVE

Kittens take their wobbly first steps when they are about three or four weeks old. Before this, they crawl around.

Wobble!

Soon, the playful kittens will be

running, chasing,

jumping,

and pouncing!

13

GROOMING

Kittens are covered in soft, fluffy fur.

Meow!

Their fur is often spotty or stripy and can be lots of different colors.
It gets thicker as they grow up.

At first, mother cats lick the kittens' fur to keep them clean. Soon, the kittens learn how to clean themselves. This is called grooming.

SUPER SENSES

Older kittens can see, smell, and hear very well. They can also feel things using their long **whiskers.**

Sight, smell, hearing, and touch are senses. They help cats and kittens find out about the world around them.

NEW HOMES

As kittens grow up, they can look after themselves better.

When they are about two or three months old, pet kittens may be ready to leave their mothers and go to new homes.

Other kittens stay with their mothers all their lives

19

GROWN-UP CATS

Most kittens are fully grown
by the time they reach
their first birthdays.
They are now
known as cats.

Grown-up female cats can have kittens of their own. They still love to play, though!

21

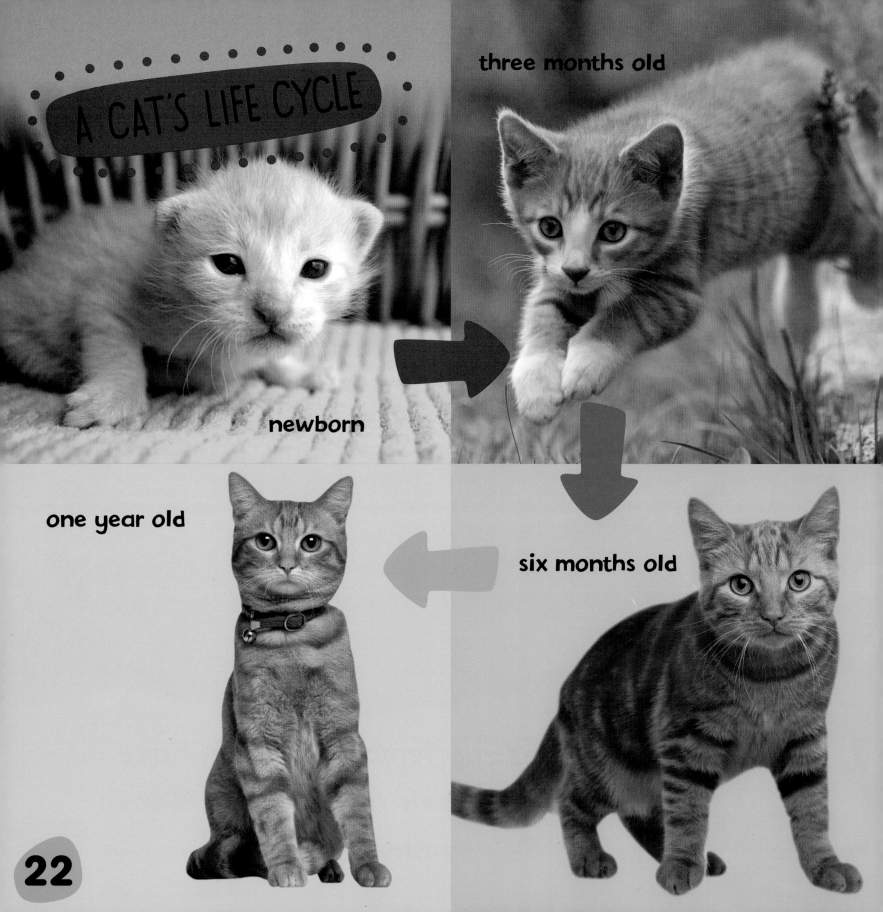

A CAT'S LIFE CYCLE

newborn

three months old

six months old

one year old

22

hiss

litter

WORD BANK

soft food

teats

whiskers

INDEX

ears, 6
eyes, 6

fur, 14–15

giving birth, 4–5
grooming, 15
grown-up cats, 20–21

keeping warm, 6

making noises, 8–9
milk, 10–11

newborns, 6–7
new homes, 19

playing, 13

senses, 6, 16–17
soft food, 11

walking, 12
whiskers, 16

Published by Smart Apple Media, an
imprint of Black Rabbit Books
P.O. Box 3263, Mankato, Minnesota 56002

U.S. publication copyright © 2017 Smart Apple Media. All
rights reserved. International copyright reserved in all
countries. No part of this book may be reproduced in any
form without written permission from the publisher.

Published by arrangement with Watts Publishing, London.

Cataloging-in-Publication Data is on file
with the Library of Congress.
ISBN: 978-1-62588-415-2
eISBN: 978-1-62588-419-0

Picture credits: Tony Campbell/Shutterstock: 14. Tatyana
Chernyah/Dreamstime: 12. John Crowe/Alamy: 4–5. Dream
Big/Shutterstock: 15. Emstudio/Shutterstock: front cover.
Alexander Ermolaev/Shutterstock: 11, 23cl. Christian
Heinrich/Imagebroker/Alamy: 13, 22tr. Isselee/Dreamstime:
20. Eric Isselee/Shutterstock: 1bl, 1tr, 22bl, 22br. Johner
Images/Alamy: 16, 23b. Juniors Bildarchiv/Alamy: 19. Andrey
Kuzmin/Shutterstock: 18. Paul McKinnon/Shutterstock: 2–3,
24. Lenar Musin/Shutterstock: 23cr. MW47/Shutterstock:
back cover tl, 7, 22tl. One Touch Spark/Dreamstime: 9,
23tl. Pavasaris1/Dreamstime: back cover tr, 21. Photo SD/
Shutterstock: 17. Evgeniya Tiplyashina/Shutterstock: 6.
Anna Utekhina/Shutterstock: 8. Rashid Valitov/Shutterstock:
10, 23tr.

Every attempt has been made to clear copyright.
Should there be any inadvertent omission please
apply to the publisher for rectification.

Printed in the United States by CG Book Printers
North Mankato, Minnesota

PO 1776

3-2016